THE
BUSINESS
OF
BELIEF

Also by Tom Asacker

Sandbox Wisdom
A Clear Eye for Branding
A Little Less Conversation
Opportunity Screams

THE
BUSINESS
OF
BELIEF

How the World's Best Marketers,
Designers, Salespeople, Coaches,
Fundraisers, Educators, Entrepreneurs
and Other Leaders Get Us to Believe

Tom Asacker

Portions of this book have appeared in somewhat different form on the author's website.

Printed in the United States of America

ISBN-10: 1483922979
ISBN-13: 978-1483922973

First Edition: 2013

Library of Congress Cataloguing in Publication Data:
A catalog record for this book is available from the Library of Congress

Cover design by Paulo Reis

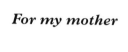

For my mother

Contents

PROLOGUE   1
CAN WE HANDLE THE TRUTH?   3

PART ONE: WHAT THEY KNOW

LIVING IS BELIEVING   7
FAIRIES ABOUND   9
WE CHOOSE THEREFORE WE BELIEVE   11
BELIEF IS A BET   13
BELIEF IS MIND-MADE   14
WE SEE WHAT WE'RE WIRED TO SEE   15
MINDS ARE MOTIVATED   17
DON'T ASK WATSON   19
BELIEF IS OPINION   20
WHOSE OPINION IS REALITY?   21
FEELINGS DIRECT ATTENTION   23
RHYME AS REASON   25
BELIEVING IS FEELING   26
CAN YOU FEEL IT?   27
MINDS MAKE MEANING   29
CLICK, WHIRR   30
MEMORY IS A CONSTRUCTION   31
WE ARE RATIONAL*IZERS*   32

BELIEF IS RELIEF   33
MEMORIES GOVERN BELIEFS   35
WE THINK IN STORIES   37
OUR STORIES STEER OUR LIVES   39
LIFE IS OUR STORY   42
ALL STORIES EVOLVE   44
MINDS CRAVE CONTROL   45
OBEDIENCE IS NOT BELIEF   47
DESIRE IS THE MARKETPLACE   49
DESIRE IS THE REASON   51
DESIRES DRIVE BELIEFS   53
BELIEVE TO ACHIEVE   54
SUMMARY OF WHAT THEY KNOW   56

PART TWO: WHAT THEY DO

UNDERSTAND OUR DESIRES AND BELIEFS   61
DESIGNING BELIEF   63
MAKE US COMFORTABLE   65
AFFECT BEFORE EFFECT   66
PAINT THE PICTURE   69
DREAMS, NOT NIGHTMARES   71
MAKE IT OURS   73
FUELING OUR FANTASY   74
MAKE IT EASY   75
AS EASY AS APPLE   77

GET US TO ACT   79
TEACHING BELIEF   80
MAKE PROGRESS VISIBLE   82
POSITIVE TICKETS   83
EXUDE PASSION   85
PASSION IS INFECTIOUS   87
CONTROL THEIR IMPULSES   89
CALM THE BATON   91
HIDE THE HOW   93
WHAT I KNOW   94
SUMMARY OF WHAT THEY DO   96

PART THREE: WHAT YOU CAN DO

BE MORE CONSCIOUS   101
THE REAL DEFINITION OF INSANITY   102
IGNORE IT   105
WHO ARE YOU?   106
FLIP YOUR LID   108
BELIEVING IS SEEING   109
BEHAVE TO BELIEVE   112
SNAP OUT OF IT!   113
STAY PASSIONATE!   116
WHAT EVER HAPPENED TO DREAMS?   119
ABOUT THE AUTHOR   123

Every man, wherever he goes, is encompassed by a cloud of comforting convictions, which move with him like flies on a summer day.

— Bertrand Russell

Prologue

I'm one lucky guy. Over the past twenty years my work has afforded me a behind the scenes look at creativity and leadership in action. I've been involved with scores of new product launches, countless branding initiatives, and some very powerful marketing campaigns.

I've helped agencies conceive ideas, travelled with skilled salespeople, advised passionate fundraisers, and worked with leaders as they've rolled out defining change initiatives. And I've confronted two realities that have redefined the nature of influence in today's modern marketplace.

The first one is this: Our choices, in all areas of life, have increased exponentially (trite but true, think cable TV). Every new product, service, cause and idea must now work overtime to capture people's attention. In my world, we refer to that reality as a "no-brainer."

The second, a fact lost on many, is that people have become very distrusting and easily distracted, making attention increasingly scarce and fleeting. Just consider the diminishing "issue-attention cycle" of critical concerns like climate change and over-population. It takes a lot of money, talent and energy to sustain people's attention, to become one of their "comforting convictions."

These conditions point to why today's most forward-looking people and organizations are moving beyond attention. They're acutely aware that it's not enough to simply have people know about them and their agendas. They need people to choose them, support them, work with them, and recommend them. In other words, they need people to believe.

Belief is an incredibly difficult concept to wrap one's head around because, like fish in water, our heads are swimming in belief. Beliefs touch every facet of our lives, mundane and profound, from the religions we choose to inform our spiritual and moral lives to the products we purchase to make us look "hot."

In fact, existence is defined by our beliefs. They determine how we feel, what we think, the goals we pursue and the actions we take. But most of us are oblivious to how beliefs are born and formed. This book is about understanding belief—what it is and how it is created. And it's about how successful people inspire and move others, or how, in my lingo, they practice the *business of belief*.

Can We Handle the Truth?

There's a Zen story about the demon Mara.
Mara is the personification of temptation and anxiety.
He seduces and frightens people.
He obscures the knowledge of ultimate truth.
Mara is referred to as "the Evil One."
One day he was traveling through a village with his posse.
He noticed a man doing walking meditation.
Suddenly, the man's face lit up in wonder.
He had come across something on the ground.
Mara's attendants were quite curious.
They asked Mara what the man had discovered.
Mara replied coolly, "It's nothing. Just a piece of truth."
"But Evil One!" exclaimed one of his entourage.
"Doesn't it bother you when someone finds a piece of the truth?"
Mara chuckled. "No. Not in the least."
"Really master? And why not?"
"Because right after they discover some truth," Mara grinned. "They usually make a belief out of it."

Part One:
What They Know

Living is Believing

Believe nothing, no matter where you read it or who has said it, not even if I have said it, unless it agrees with your own reason and your own common sense.

— Buddha

Siddhartha Gautama Buddha lived over 2,500 years ago in what is now Nepal. A land of tribal people living in territorial monarchies. People who didn't spend much time shopping, who rarely travelled outside their kingdoms, and who never puzzled over their choices of information, media or entertainment. It was quite possible for most of them to heed Siddhartha's sage advice and consciously consider their varied beliefs.

Today it's impossible. Our modern marketplace has morphed into a dizzying kaleidoscope revealing a surfeit of choice. When I searched Amazon.com's book section for "buddha," I was presented with 16,161 options. Try "reasoning" your way through that list (and as search results go, it's a relatively short tally).

It's certainly possible to limit our choices, to slow down and be more mindful of everyday decisions, but unless you're a monk your pre-frontal cortex will ultimately be overwhelmed. The human brain was not designed to dispassionately evaluate today's innumerable options. If you tried, you'd end up like this unfortunate invertebrate:

A centipede was happy quite,
Until a frog in fun
Said, "Pray which leg comes after which?"
This raised her mind to such a pitch,
She lay distracted in a ditch
Considering how to run.

So, how do we choose? What they know that you may not is that we choose what we choose because we believe in it. And those beliefs are (or were) driven by our desires.

To appreciate this powerful peculiarity of human nature—to understand how and why it happens—is to better know how to motivate yourself, make better decisions, and create conditions so that others will motivate themselves to choose you.

Fairies Abound

Arthur Conan Doyle was a 19th century physician.
He studied medicine at the University of Edinburgh.
He completed his doctorate at age 26.
Doyle also liked to write stories.
Especially when business was slow at his medical practice.
During that time he created Sherlock Holmes.
The world's greatest detective.
The most rational character in literature.
More logical than Mr. Spock.
Doyle clearly had a handle on critical thinking.
He also believed in fairies.
Little, people-like spirits.
How could the author of the quintessentially rational Sherlock Holmes believe in winged, magical creatures?
Doyle became a devotee of Spiritualism.
A popular religion that believed the dead continue to exist in the world as spirits.
A belief system that erroneously "proved" religious claims of an afterlife.
Since spirits exist, there must be life after death.

Doyle desperately wanted this to be true.

He tragically lost his first wife to tuberculosis.

The Great War then took his brother-in-law, two nephews and several other friends and relatives.

Doyle was eventually driven into depression by the deaths of his son and brother in the flu epidemic.

His immersion into Spiritualism may have been his lift ticket out.

No one knew for sure.

Not even Sir Arthur Conan Doyle.

But his behavior changed.

His involvement in the movement intensified.

He travelled the world.

He followed the research and attended seances.

He wrote articles and books and began lecturing for the cause.

He collected a huge number of spirit photographs, including a now famous one of fairies in Cottingly.

He also received a great deal of criticism and lost many friends, including the magician Harry Houdini.

Such is the nature of belief.

So what is it that you believe?

What do you want to be true?

We Choose Therefore We Believe

Belief is what humans do. Our personal beliefs define our choices, shape our lives and, collectively, determine our futures. Nothing is more important than belief. If you want to change the world, if you want to change *your* world, if you want to succeed at work, in the marketplace, or in any other social endeavor or organization, belief is your Holy Grail.

Take a quick mental run through yesterday morning's decisions. What brand of toothpaste did you use? Did you drink coffee or tea? Which sweetener did you stir into it? Did you eat breakfast? Bacon and eggs? Fruit and yogurt? Did you take any vitamins? Which ones? Did you watch the news? Which network?

Keep going. Did you workout? What brand of running shoe did you lace up? Did you run? Lift weights? Do yoga? Did you drive to work or take public transportation? What kind of vehicle did you drive? Gas-powered? Electric? Hybrid-electric? Which morning radio show did you tune into? Did you text while driving? Did you buckle up? Did you light up?

Whether your decisions were consciously considered or habitual, they were decisions nonetheless. And you made them because you wanted to—perhaps they were quick or easy, or they scratched an itch or validated a previous decision. In any case, you believed, for reasons known or unknown to you, that they were the right decisions for you to make, at that time.

Beliefs are really nothing more than working assumptions. Most are provisional, conditional and have varying degrees of certainty—"I know I'm not very creative. I think that walnuts are good for heart health. I'm pretty sure that our organization is making a difference. I'm positive the Earth is round."

We make life's most trivial and most meaningful decisions according to those assumptions. And we weigh them by holding desire in one hand and by placing our sketchy assessment of the risks and uncertainties (which typically carry more weight) in the other.

It seems simple, and it is. But how and why our minds work to create and nourish our beliefs is quite curious and largely invisible to us.

Many adolescents suffer from mood swings.

Causes range from chemical imbalances in the body to environmental factors like stress.

Those with severe, disruptive mood swings are commonly treated with drugs.

That's one of today's working assumptions.

When I was growing up, psychosurgery was a mainstream treatment for mood swings.

Prefrontal lobotomy.

A physician would shock the disturbed patient into unconsciousness.

Then insert an ice-pick like tool through the eye socket, tap it with a hammer, and swirl it around.

Viola! Offending neural connections effectively scrambled in a little under ten minutes.

John F. Kennedy's older sister Rosie was lobotomized and totally incapacitated when she was 23.

Tragically, so was Tennessee Williams' beloved sister.

Would you allow such barbaric treatment of your moody child?

Would you be willing to make that bet?

Not today.

Belief is Mind-Made

"Believing seems the most mental thing we do," wrote Bertrand Russell in 1921. Yet for all of our discoveries in the fields of cognitive psychology, computer science, behavioral economics and neuroscience, the process of belief remains an utter mystery. There is no universally accepted mental representation of the belief concept.

And there never will be. Because belief is unique and fluid. Belief is a personal construct, an emotionally-colored fusion of imperfect mental processes like perception and memory. Our beliefs are influenced and reinforced by a host of idiosyncratic factors, including our present circumstances, our mood and personality.

It's difficult to appreciate, but our minds don't reflect reality, like a mirror. Reality is an abstraction and reconstruction. We create it from our sensations and impressions, colored by our past experiences and our unique understanding of facts and events. When the Jesuit priest Anthony de Mello wrote, "We see people and things not as they are, but as we are," he was describing belief.

We See What We're Wired to See

Back in my university days, my roommate called and
urged me to come witness some type of faith healer.
It was a slow night, so I rushed to the venue.
I watched as a mysterious man cut a gash in his
thumb with a pocket knife.
He then healed it under cover of a borrowed scarf.
He even let my friend hold the radial artery of his
arm, while he miraculously "willed" his pulse rate to
zero.
My pre-med friend was awestruck.
He talked about it during the entire, freezing cold
walk home.
But I finally shut him up.
When we arrived at our room, I covertly snagged the
requisite prop (a tennis ball).
Then I made *my* pulse stop in precisely the same
way.
We were both intelligent, well-educated
underclassmen.
But we had very different mental wiring.
Part of mine was formed during many solitary hours
practicing close-up magic.

And so my mind was primed to see what was literally invisible to him.

On that particular night, and every night since, we experienced different realities.

Minds are Motivated

Psychology and social science experiments have repeatedly established the human brain's seemingly irrational behavior—incorrect assumptions, improper assessments, and inappropriate choices. But the word "irrational" belies the fact that, unlike a passionless computer, a brain is motivated. It desires —to conserve energy and make guesses, to avoid loss, to be liked and accepted, to appear consistent.

To paraphrase Forrest Gump, rational is what rational wants. Reason is simply a tool to help the brain get what it cares about (and to feel good about it). And a brain cares, first and foremost, about itself —what's happening in its environment and why, how it appears (to others and to itself), and whether or not it's safe and in control.

These hardwired biases to see patterns and make meaning, craft an acceptable and consistent personal narrative, and exert control over its environment are the irresistible forces that influence the brain's creation of beliefs.

Despite today's prevailing computer metaphor, your brain is not a fleshy machine (prior analogies have included electromagnets, combustion engines and a water clock). Machines are cold, predictable and soulless.

Your brain is a living, pulsating tangle of nerve fibers. A self-organizing network of trillions of connections, customized by genetics, upbringing, expectations and experiences. Like the underground root system of a plant, it's growing and changing.

But, unlike a plant, your brain selects and modifies all input and makes its own, subjective sense of things. It infuses your memory with personal meaning, alerts you, primarily, to what might harm you, and draws you toward what's exciting and pleasurable.

It's powerful, but insecure. It's fast, but error prone. It's clever, but extremely lazy. It sees a lot, but ignores infinitely more. The brain, as Emily Dickinson so beautifully described it, "is wider than the Sky," and yet it also makes us feel like isolated egos inside bags of skin.

Don't Ask Watson

In 2011, a supercomputer named Watson beat two of
"Jeopardy's" most successful human champions.
Watson's fifteen developers spent more than 3 years
and $3 million in hardware to pull off that feat.
Watson is not your run-of-the-mill machine.
It's one of the world's greatest question answerers.
But don't ask Watson if you should start a business.
It won't have a clue.
And don't ask Watson how to paint the night sky
with the brilliance of Van Gogh.
Or how to create moving poetry like Rilke, or inspire
the masses like Jesus.
And certainly don't ask Watson if you should set
yourself on fire to protest corruption.
Or throw yourself in front of an oncoming vehicle to
save the life of a stranger.
As someone once said (and no, it wasn't Einstein),
"Computers are incredibly fast, accurate and stupid.
Human beings are incredibly slow, inaccurate and
brilliant.
Together they are powerful beyond imagination."
Let us never confuse the two.

Belief is Opinion

While delivering the commencement speech at Yale University in 1962, President John F. Kennedy noted, "We subject all facts to a prefabricated set of interpretations. We enjoy the comfort of opinion without the discomfort of thought. Mythology distracts us everywhere."

Our individual mythologies, our comfortable, prefabricated interpretations and sets of opinions, *are* our beliefs. Whether it's what clothes to wear, vehicle to drive, school to attend, or charity to support, where to live, what to eat, how to pray, or for whom to vote, it's all part of a powerful, personal narrative—an evolving story of who we believe we are, how we believe we should behave, and why.

This book is about that story, about how our value judgments are formed, for better or for worse, and about how others influence them, for good or for bad. It's about what belief is, why it happens, and what it does.

Whose Opinion is Reality?

Sixto Rodriguez was born in the summer of 1942 to working-class immigrants in Detroit, Michigan.

For the past forty years, he's barely scraped by doing backbreaking labor and living in a dilapidated house.

During that same time, Rodriguez was also a rock star.

More popular than the Beatles or the Rolling Stones.

That's the fervent opinion of millions.

In the late 60s, the once aspiring singer-songwriter cut a couple of albums.

They were commercial flops in the United States.

His dreams dashed, Rodriguez spent the rest of his life hustling for odd jobs in Detroit's inner city.

Meanwhile his first album somehow made it to South Africa in the early 70s.

An oppressive regime ripe for its poetic protest songs.

And so it caught fire and became the soundtrack of the anti-Apartheid movement.

And Rodriguez morphed into a mythological musical icon.

Sixto Rodriguez, a workaday laborer from Detroit? Or Rodriguez, a one-of-a-kind folk rock hero. What you believe depends on where you are (and when).

Feelings Direct Attention

Recent theories in human judgment and decision-making, shaped by psychological and neuroscientific research by academics like Daniel Kahneman and António Damásio, are confirming what philosophers from Plato through Descartes and beyond have known to be true: We are of two minds. And, as the Scottish philosopher David Hume rightly postulated, it's our intuitive, "feeling" mind that directs our more analytical, "thinking" mind. Our gut, rather than our head, steers our attention and behavior.

Let's say you're hiking up a hot and rocky desert trail, just as the sun is beginning to set, when you suddenly notice an ambiguous, twisted brown object protruding from the shadowy rocks and brushing up against your bare leg. What do you do? You certainly don't bend your face towards it to get a closer look. You jump back! You make the meaning first —"Snake!"—and only later, if it matters to you, do you assess that belief.

That's how our brains evolved—by seeking patterns and making meaning, everywhere and all the time.

We see animals in wind-blown bushes and in random cloud formations, faces in crowds and on the moon, and prophecy in science fiction and in ancient calendars. We believe we know people's feelings based on their email responses or facial expressions. We imagine how something will taste by its appearance. We hear a loud bang! and reflexively duck for cover.

Sometimes connecting the dots aids us in making predictions, like when cloud formations foretell impending storms or a funky smell stops us from pouring milk on our cereal. At other times, we make causal associations that are baseless. Our feeling mind has a really tough time knowing the difference.

You wear a wristband and find that your balance has improved—"It's the ions!" You're giving a speech and notice the room go eerily quiet—"I've lost them." You lose five hands of blackjack in a row —"I'm unlucky."

In fact, the wristband may have simply triggered your mind to slow down and be more conscious of your golf swing, your reserved audience may be engaged in reflective thought, and, like many other gambling games, blackjack is won and lost in streaks.

Rhyme as Reason

In the book "Thinking, Fast and Slow," there's an
example of intuition bias that makes me smile.
And there's another one that concerns me.
Here's the first one.
"A bat and a ball cost $1.10 in total.
The bat costs $1 more than the ball.
How much does the ball cost?"
Did you think "10 cents?"
Most people do, because it *feels* right.
But it's wrong, and that's okay.
And here's the one that worries me.
Which is more accurate?
"Woes unite foes," or "Woes unite enemies."
A much-cited study found the first statement easier
to process and therefore more believable.
Because it rhymes!
During his closing statement to the jury, O.J.
Simpson's lawyer made a declarative statement.
"If the glove doesn't fit, you must acquit."
Attorney Cochran was either very lucky or
deviously smart.

Believing is Feeling

So yes, our intuition, our impulsive feeling mind, can lead us astray. But it leads us, nonetheless. It directs our attention, informs our beliefs and guides our reflections and decisions. And when it is proven right, through experience or analysis, we have reinforcing evidence of the value of those beliefs. Our perception becomes our reality, and a belief is born.

Your beliefs are what make the external world appear so convincingly real to you. Everything feels so stable, orderly and predictable. But it's not. Your perception of reality is really an elaborate construction. A psychological model that continuously draws upon context, memories and desires to simulate a cohesive whole.

It's the greatest illusion in the world, and the most difficult one to dispel. Because, no matter how well it's described, you simply can not see it or feel it. And yet that illusion—your unique perspective—conditions your sensibilities and beliefs. And ultimately, it drives your decisions.

Can You Feel It?

Do you believe you're an outgrowth of a living
sphere?
A huge mass rocketing through space faster than a
bullet shot out of a gun around another ball of fire?
You may know it, but you don't *feel* it.
If you did—and I mean deep in your bones—it
would profoundly change the way you live your life.
Or consider that your body is inhabited by trillions
of bacteria.
As much as six pounds of your bodyweight.
Living organisms that stimulate your immune
system, allow you to digest foods, and produce
vitamins and anti-inflammatory molecules.
You'd cease to exist without them (and vice-versa).
I'll bet you believe the Earth is round.
Because your mind *feels* that the world is round.
You've been told over and over again that it's round.
And the models in schools and photographs from
space make it appear round.
But it's not. It's a bumpy, oblate spheroid.
Many years ago, people *felt* that the Earth was flat.

And so they refused to sail out to the "edge" for fear of falling off.

Can you believe it?

You can if you can *feel* it.

Minds Make Meaning

You enter your hotel bathroom and notice a triangle folded in the toilet tissue. What does it mean? All you really *know* is that someone folded a triangle in the toilet paper. But your mind searches its inventory for a similar pattern, finds it, and completes the picture to envision someone cleaning the room, making the bed, and performing other tasks consistent with your memories of that particular experience.

Your brain works like an elaborate and evolving "connect the dots" puzzle. New information and experiences create new dots, new neural connections, which make your mental pictures of the world richer and more insightful.

But here's the trouble with that system: Whether or not your mental dots actually form a credible picture is irrelevant. Your mind simply wants to understand and make predictions. So it will invent dots until it envisions a coherent picture. This happens automatically and the resulting view is the unique, imaginative frame through which you look at the world.

If I say, "It was a dark and stormy."
You connect the dots and think "night."
But why didn't you think "cocktail?"
After all, there is a drink called "Dark and Stormy."
It's made with dark rum, ginger beer and lime.
If you're driving and a ball comes flying across the
road in front of you (click), your mind thinks
(whirr), "Kid!"
A similar process arises when you're first exposed to
a website, an advertisement or a salesperson.
Your present passes through a filter of your past to
create spontaneous meaning.
When you see the word "swastika," what meaning
do you create?
"Swastika" comes from the Sanskrit "svastika."
It literally means, "to be good."
It's a good luck symbol.
But in 1920 it was adopted by the Nazi Party.
And now the click of "swastika" creates an
emotional whirr of hate.
Everything is inherently without meaning.
Except for the meaning we create.

Memory is a Construction

When my friend and I experienced the "healer," we each witnessed something different. That's because what we see depends on what we believe—on how our minds are wired with information and experiences. We only see what we're prepared to see, and what we expect to experience influences what we do experience.

Despite how it may feel, your mind doesn't record each and every detail of your experiences, and then project them back to you on an inner screen. Rather, you select and interpret patterns from your singular point of view, store them as experiences and associations (dots), and later reconstruct them on-the-spot.

After I showed my friend the healer's tricks, he revised his mental picture of the experience. He created a new memory and a new reality. However, there are times when we hold tight to our memories and beliefs, even in the face of disconfirming evidence. And this usually occurs when they have been infused with emotion and personal relevance.

I recently watched an interview with Bob Dylan.
He unequivocally stated that he never wrote songs
as a commentary on social or political events.
I don't believe him.
Why not?
Because my memories of his poetic lyrics embody
my sensibilities.
Many of which were formed during the social unrest
of the Sixties.
And I'm not about to give up those feelings, that
"Bob Dylan" part of my identity (we even share the
same birthday).
When I think about it, I recognize that my belief is
irrational.
And so I choose not to think about it.
I've relieved my mental tension by conjuring up my
own reasons for Dylan's distortion.
With that particular belief, and with many others
that are hidden away from my conscious awareness,
I choose to rational*ize* rather than be rational.
So do you.
We all do.

Belief is Relief

Our minds crave consistency in our beliefs and behaviors. We want to appear logical, to ourselves and to others. And when faced with evidence which contradicts our beliefs, our minds work to eliminate the psychological discomfort.

We typically achieve this mental relief in one of three ways. We suppress the conflicting thought or down-play its importance—"Dylan was just playing it up for the camera, like he frequently does." We outweigh the conflicting thought with ones which are consistent with our beliefs—"If he didn't really *feel* the issues of the times, Dylan could have never written songs like that." Or we change our beliefs —"Not me! And, for what it's worth, I don't care what the Beatles claimed either. *Lucy in the Sky with Diamonds* was about L.S.D."

Making decision after decision, large and small, in the face of countless options, conflicting viewpoints and unknown consequences requires a lifetime of tuning out cognitive dissonance. That's why we love the relief of discovering that it's healthy to be slightly overweight or to consume a few alcoholic beverages each day. It's why we boldly tell ourselves that it's okay for us to smoke cigarettes, since our grandparents smoked and both lived into their 90s. And it's why we gladly end the "paper or plastic" conundrum by assuring ourselves that it's trivial, or by toting our own canvas bags.

Choice is liberating, and belief flourishes with the freedom to choose. But every choice also chains us, because it rejects a world brimming with competing opinions and possibilities. Our believing minds simply can not function while brooding over all of those chains. The psychic strain would paralyze us. And so we ignore them.

In most cases, we look for and find confirmatory evidence in support of our beliefs. In others, we invent our own "proof," like I did with Dylan. Or we close our minds to conflicting points of view, which is the sad state of affairs in modern day politics. In any case, we almost always find a way to create a story that reinforces what we want to believe.

Memories Govern Beliefs

I swallow handfuls of dietary supplements.
Everything from vitamin D to fish oil and turmeric.
I've been trained to suspect health claims, so I
should have a grasp on the origins of my regimen.
But I don't.
I've never seen empirical evidence that supports the
benefits of any of it (and I don't even feel any
effects).
I must have strung a bunch of memories together to
form a compelling story.
A *re*presentation of my experiences.
Those "dots" probably include media mentions and
recommendations from friends.
Plus some knowledge of medical history, and choice
memories from my time running a medical company.
There may even be one flashback of the genius Ray
Kurzweil gobbling down supplements in a
documentary movie.
I've recently read that taking supplements is not
only unnecessary in most cases, but may be
dangerous.

But that one "dot" is not strong enough to disengage my well-connected mental image.

It's simply a possibility.

One that I presently choose to ignore.

We Think in Stories

Storytelling is all the rage in business today. But storytelling is far more than an engaging form of information transfer or an addictive form of entertainment. It's how we make sense of the world.

The job of the conscious mind is to automatically produce a story to make sense out of our perceptions and reflections. Those stories—or schemas, metaphors and mental models—are how we connect the abstract content of our minds into recognizable patterns. And the easier it is for our minds to conjure a pattern, to make a particular association, the more confidence we have in our invented story.

When we enter that hotel bathroom and see the triangle folded in the toilet tissue, we create a cleanliness story. When Mr. Whipple implores us in a TV ad, "Please don't squeeze the Charmin," it activates a story of softness. Christina Aguilera's platinum blonde hair and bright red lipstick evoke a Marilyn Monroe story. Apple's elegant and thoughtful packaging conjures up a story of quality and craftsmanship.

All stories—heard, read or invented—actively engage our inner lives where we form our own, vivid and personally relevant adaptations. To the mind, these imagined experiences are processed as real ones—the very same neurons are being connected and activated. And this brain engagement is far more powerful and influential than you could possibly imagine.

Athletes and salespeople create inner experiences that, like actual practice, help them perform at peak levels. Wine geeks create stories, which cause their minds to prefer the taste of wine from an expensive bottle to the exact same wine from a lower priced one. Generic chocolate labeled "Swiss" tastes better than the same chocolate labeled "Made in China." And, strangely, we believe that little "Scrubbing Bubble" guys are actually helping us clean our tubs.

Like moths to a flame, we're instinctively drawn by our desires to a plethora of choices. And the motivation for our decisions are driven by the vivid narratives we spontaneously create. Our brains have evolved to work that way, to transform reality by making up cause and effect stories.

Our Stories Steer Our Lives

I recently read a fascinating study where researchers gave participants the ability to fly using virtual reality.

Some were passengers in a helicopter.

Others flew under their own power with arms extended.

The people who flew like "Superman" were later more likely to provide help to others in the real world.

The theory is that their inner experiences inspired them to embody the role of superhero.

Without them having the slightest clue.

It sounds crazy, but I believe it.

I know, first hand, the power of stories.

I wrote my first book more than a decade ago.

I got the idea while sitting unemployed and downhearted at my breakfast table.

As I stared blankly into my coffee cup, I caught a glimpse of my youngest daughter playing with her spoon.

She was gazing into it with a puzzled look on her face.

Then she flipped it around and raised her eyebrows.

"Honey, what *are* you doing?" I asked.

"Daddy? How come this way, I'm upside down?
But when I turn it around, I'm right side up?!"
She waited anxiously for a response.

I sat speechless.

I knew the words "convex" and "concave," but I had
no idea why her spoon reflection was flipping (I still
don't).

However, that simple question set my mind in
motion.

I imagined a story about business.

About how people knew a lot of fancy concepts, but
not much about the real lives of the people they
serve.

Then I conjured up another story, with me as the
protagonist who exposes the Emperor's nakedness.

And then another, with me writing a book and
standing on stage speaking to large groups of
people.

My self-deceptive mind was on one heck of a roll.

And, thankfully, it's been rolling along ever since.

But most of us forget.

There was a time when our minds were *always* on a
roll.

We used boxes and sticks to become astronauts and artists.

We created fantasy characters and outrageous worlds.

We drew whimsical pictures and cooked up wild ideas.

We were complete originals.

And some of us, the ones with the most vivid stories, became today's inventors, poets, actors, and musicians.

Stories are powerful.

Because we all become the stories we tell ourselves.

Life is Our Story

The British psychologist Richard Gregory wrote, "The senses do not give us a picture of the world directly; rather they provide evidence for the checking of hypotheses about what lies before us."

Those hypotheses, those beliefs, are conditioned by the stories we tell ourselves—stories that have been sewn into the roots of our consciousness by upbringing, culture, education and experience. And especially by the meanings we ascribe to each one—meanings which have a meta-meaning we call "self" or "me," the chief character at the center of our evolving story.

Look back over your life and it will appear as orderly, consistent, and sentimental as a composed narrative. We describe periods of our lives as if they were "chapters"—like our sandlot years and college days—and with specific "actors" and defining "scenes." That's because our minds were wired to create meaning and structure out of a fragmented and complicated tangle of connections, to string random twists and turns into a causally-linked set of events.

Emerson once remarked that there is properly no history, only biography. The stories we create about the past aren't the Truth (with a capital T). They're a personal fiction, the mind's meaning-making apparatus at work. But, like most everything the mind creates, it affects us. How we visualize each role in each scene not only shapes how we think about ourselves, but also how we behave. Who we think we are is why we do what we do.

We live in our stories, and we live according to them. We wear clothing and drive vehicles, which are consistent with who we believe we are and who we are trying to become. We choose relationships and information as ways of subconsciously validating our beliefs, to make us feel good about our points of view. Our treasured books and music embody us. Our closest friends are our kind of people.

Ultimately, we expect to find meaning in our lives by editing our stories, by freely mixing and matching our decisions to create an authentic narrative that represents who we believe we are, to ourselves and to others. And one of the key elements of that creation process is our desire to control it, to be inner-directed and free of influence.

I saw a short video about the documentary
filmmaker Ken Burns.
He was talking about his formula for a great story
and brought up his award-winning series "Baseball."
Specifically the part about the great Jackie Robinson.
Robinson was the first African-American to play in
the major leagues.
He debuted with the Brooklyn Dodgers in 1947.
A time of mounting racial tension and intolerance.
Burns noted, "It seemed to me that there was a
dilemma for the racist of what to do about Jackie
Robinson.
If you were a Brooklyn Dodger fan, and you were a
racist, what do you do when he arrives?
You can quit baseball, all together.
You can change teams.
Or, you can . . . change."
In 1947, Jackie Robinson was a force on the Dodgers'
diamond and in America's hearts and minds.
His story, as a cultural icon, was set.
Die-hard racist fans had no other option.
Theirs had to evolve.

Minds Crave Control

Our desire to direct our own stories is more than the universal hunger for autonomy, for freedom of choice. It's a profound psychological need to feel powerful and in control of our lives and our environment.

Have you ever created a story about some aspect of your life and later discovered that someone lied to you, making it all a distressing illusion? When we experience this sudden powerlessness, it can feel devastating. And that's because we've temporarily lost control of our narrative. We don't know where we're heading, or who or what to believe.

On the other hand if we believe we know what's happening around us, especially the near term future and general direction, we feel safe. That's why we resist change and want our agendas and ideologies to prevail. It gives us the comforting feeling of knowing how things will turn out, assuring us that we have the knowledge and experience to survive and, hopefully, to thrive.

Of course, control is an illusion. Most of what happens in life has little to do with our conscious decisions. We are being pushed and pulled by our environment and our instincts. But we imagine otherwise. We create a meaning-infused narrative to rationalize that we are autonomous, powerful individuals—free to be ourselves and entitled to be treated with respect.

Let me be clear: Power *is* shifting from the large and authoritarian to the individual. The Internet has unleashed our freedom to choose by providing copious information, ever-expanding options, and an increasing degree of active involvement in our decision-making. But this full participation is as likely to create stress as satisfaction, as we trust less and assume more and more responsibility.

What "they" know is this: We don't really want total control and responsibility. We want guided control—based on an empathetic assessment of our feelings and desires—along with the freedom to create our own meaning, our own story, without external pressure or coercion. What we want is the *illusion* of control.

Obedience is Not Belief

Many are aware of the controversial obedience
experiment performed by Stanley Milgram.
The one where volunteers gave people pretending to
be subjects increasingly powerful electric shocks.
Shocks that the volunteers believed were causing the
subjects pain, agony and even death (they weren't).
It's a disturbing look into the power of authority.
But there's more to the story.
It started out with a domineering man in a lab coat.
He made it very clear to the volunteers that they
were part of pioneering research at Yale University.
An important and worthy study on the effects of
punishment on learning.
Once the volunteers understood and agreed, once
they *believed*, the experimenter began the "study."
His role was to goad volunteers to shock subjects
whenever the "learners" got an answer wrong.
And to continue to shock them, with increasing
voltage, for each wrong answer.
Whenever a volunteer would struggle or resist, the
experimenter would use four sequential verbal
prods.

"Please go on."

"The experiment requires that you continue."

"It's absolutely essential that you continue."

"You have no other choice, you must go on."

Despite expressing feelings that it was wrong, 65%
of the volunteers inflicted the maximum voltage.

Even when subjects were screaming in agony.

Some subjects even feigned loss of consciousness.

It was quite disturbing.

But something interesting happened at the final
prod.

When the experimenter would say, "You have no
other choice, you must go on," no one did.

Not one single volunteer.

They were willing to inflict, and endure, suffering
for what they were led to *believe* was a worthy cause.

But only when they felt they had control.

The minute they were issued an order, they stopped.

Of course people can be forced to follow an order.

But the need to do so reveals something.

It means they don't believe in it.

And so eventually they will resist.

No one can be forced to believe.

Belief depends upon the freedom to choose.

Desire is the Marketplace

We have become enamored with independence, autonomy, and the freedom to choose, to be the authors of our lives. This liberation of the self has brought with it a corresponding explosion of desire. And it's this outburst of intention that has animated the marketplace.

When I asked you earlier to reflect on yesterday morning's beliefs, what I was ultimately after was a list of your desires. Some of those desires were formed as the result of a deliberate thought process —perhaps you had an important meeting and desired to dress to impress. Others simply popped into your head, seemingly out of nowhere— Pancakes!

You may be thinking, "Wait a minute. I certainly made decisions that I didn't desire, like flossing my teeth." That's simply not true. To be fully aware is to recognize that there is no distinction between what you do and what you desire. If you flossed your teeth, you were motivated to floss. You may not have been aware of it, but desire is, or was, the trigger that moved you.

Desires are constantly being stimulated and reinforced by outside forces and life circumstances. They can spring unknowingly from your feeling mind, driven by your wanting, in the moment, to feel good or avoid feeling bad—like quenching a thirst. Or they can bubble up into your thinking mind as you impulsively contemplate your options —a glass of water or head to the drive-through for a large iced mocha latte?

In any event, desire is the spark that ignites your beliefs and fuels your actions. The most important thing "they" know is this: although your thinking mind is skilled at estimating and comparing options, your feeling mind is the crew chief. If it doesn't desire what the thinking mind is contemplating, nothing will happen. Desire is what moves you from thinking to doing.

And that's why all the information in the world will not get people to quit smoking, start exercising, or end an unhealthy relationship. If our hearts are not into it, if we don't truly desire the change, our heads won't be either. We are not computers. We don't optimize our decisions. We decide, and believe, in order to feel good. And to avoid feeling bad.

Desire is the Reason

I remember a funny, yet sad episode of the television police drama "NYPD Blue."

It featured a man selling black boxes to plain-looking women, promising them an improved appearance.

All they had to do was plug it in and wear it over their heads for a few hours each day.

And pay him $2,000.

The story sounds like the preposterous invention of a comedic screenwriter, but it's not really.

For years, I've seen ads for a unique brand of fitness equipment that looks like a Victorian time machine.

It allows you to "Exercise in exactly 4 minutes per day!"

And in those few minutes, you can get the same results as an hour and a half of conventional exercise.

For a little over $14,000.

Interestingly, the ads show up in the back of popular science magazines, which appeal to "rational" readers.

People who believe in things, as long as there's a reason and evidence to believe them.

Whether those readers are aware of it or not, desire is their reason to believe.

And evidence is their permission.

Just like the "irrational" women who wore the black boxes.

Desires Drive Beliefs

Desire not only focuses our attention on what's attractive—on what has the potential to make us feel good—but also on information that supports those feelings. If we desire something, we'll be attentive to the evidence that supports it and inattentive to conflicting evidence. And we update our beliefs based on that biased data.

Aspiring writers, athletes, actors and musicians ignore the mountain of data that point to frustration in their pursuits of fame and fortune. Instead, they persist by focusing on spoonsful of evidence—recognition, signs of progress and emotionally charged hero stories—which support their beliefs.

The same is true of entrepreneurs and others risk takers. Desire fuels belief, especially in their ability to control their destiny, and through thoughtful and determined action (and luck) many achieve what they put their minds to. Belief, then, is a somewhat naïve, self-fulfilling prophecy. Desire drives belief, which motivates people to seek out information and act in certain ways that help them attain those desires.

In 1988, two psychologists published an article
making a somewhat disturbing argument.
They claimed that positive self-deception is a normal
and beneficial part of most people's lives.
It turns out that we lie to ourselves about three
things.
We view ourselves in implausibly positive ways.
We think we have far more control over our lives
than we actually do.
And we believe that the future will be better than the
evidence of the present can possibly justify.
These positive illusions help us feel good about
ourselves and our decisions.
Just ask Spencer West.
His mind was motivated to ignore his legs.
Or more precisely his lack of legs, which were
amputated below the pelvis when he was just five.
Spencer simply wanted to raise funds for a Kenyan
charity.
By scaling Africa's highest mountain.
And so, after a year of training, he completed the
grueling climb up Mount Kilimanjaro in seven days.

Using only his hands.

Whether you believe you can or you believe you can't, you're probably right.

Summary of What They Know

We live in a world where we're free to choose what we believe. The marketplace has responded to our independence—and desire for stimulation and self-expression—with a corresponding outpouring of new products, causes and ideas. This flood of options has overwhelmed our very limited cognitive abilities.

We certainly have the freedom to choose among the options we perceive to be available to us, but our ability to exercise that freedom—to be consciously aware of our choices and to rationally evaluate them —is derailed by our nature, acculturation and modern day circumstances.

It's difficult, in fact almost impossible to conceive but we don't really know why we do most of what we do. Our mind's influence on most of our decisions is outside of our conscious experience. Instead, we're being pulled by our instincts—by our desires and our interactions with the world—and we relieve the tension of our imperfect choices, of our beliefs, by persuading ourselves that given our character and circumstances they're the right ones for us to make.

Our minds abhor a causality vacuum. We have a deep desire to understand and explain everything to ourselves, including the random twist and turns of our own lives. When no explanation is forthcoming, we will instinctively make one up to suit our situation and disposition, to make us feel good about our decisions and our stories.

Our desires and evolving personal narratives focus our attention. We choose people, things, information, and experiences that reinforce our worldview and bolster our self-esteem, and we look for, and find, evidence to help us rationalize those decisions.

Our rational mind has a mind of its own—a feeling mind—whose decisions are biased by various motivations, limitations, and, especially, social influences. These biases help us navigate a demanding and complex world, keep our personal narratives meaningful and consistent, and engender acceptance and approval of the people around us.

What we believe is what we desire, and what we desire is ultimately what we do. It's the human condition.

Part Two:
What They Do

Understand Our Desires and Beliefs

Changing a belief is like crossing a footbridge stretched above a deep chasm; it requires motivation (a reason) and consideration (evidence). Life presents us with a myriad of these bridges. Most are short, clear and relatively stable, like choosing a new wine in return for a novel experience.

But there are also long, dark and rickety ones, like launching a new career or participating in a major change initiative. Only those who truly desire what's on the other side, and who feel relatively safe and in control, will be moved to venture across.

Those skilled at motivating people to cross a new bridge, to change their beliefs and behavior, are not trying to cajole or manipulate them against their will. Rather, they seek to guide them to a new destination, a transformed way of feeling, thinking and acting that's aligned with their personal desires and values.

At its core, then, altering someone's beliefs is not an act of short-lived persuasion; it's an act of leadership (the root of the word "lead" means "to go forth, to travel.") And every leader knows that before you can lead people, you have to know where they *want* to go. *Want* is not the same impulse as need, nor is it simply a wish or a dream. Want, or desire, is a motivating force which shapes our choices. We need food, but we may want vegan or organic. We wish we were rich, but we may desire a stable and relatively stress-free job. Effective leaders understand this distinction and draw powerful inferences from it.

Howard Schultz turned around Starbucks by soliciting advice from its enthusiastic employees and customers, and by acting on those desires and beliefs with a host of new products and experiences. Steve Jobs imagined the iPod and iTunes by connecting his deep involvement in technology and design with an in-depth knowledge of the wants of consumers, as well as the fears and desires of the music industry. Mahatma Gandhi felt the oppression of his fellow Indians and, equally important, he was keenly aware of the desires and beliefs of the colonial authorities.

Effective leaders know that the essential first step to changing people's behavior is to understand *their* perspectives and embrace *their* desires and beliefs. Everything else flows naturally from there.

Designing Belief

When I first heard of it, I thought it was a "Saturday Night Live" parody product.

Yet since it hit the international market in 2007, devout Muslim women have been snapping them up.

It's called the "Burkini" (an oxymoronic combination of Burka and bikini).

Stylish and comfortable swimwear that also meets the Islamic requirements for modesty.

The idea was conceived by a Lebanese Australian woman.

She was inspired by watching her Muslim niece struggle to play netball in bulky covering.

And so she designed a new belief.

One that resonated her audience's values and desires.

In retrospect, the idea seems obvious.

But that's true of many new beliefs.

A horseless carriage? Sounds ridiculous.

Flying machines? Really?

A Star Trek-like communication device? C'mon.

A driverless car?

Dieter Rams said good designers "must have an intuition for the reality in which people live.
For their dreams, their desires, their worries, their needs, their living habits."
Great designers design new beliefs.

Make Us Comfortable

Once leaders discover our beliefs, they probe deeply to uncover what's in, and on, our minds—the images, words and symbols that attract, inspire and motivate us. With these deep insights as their guide, they develop communication and experiences to join with those primed connections and create familiar and motivating meaning.

Imagine people inching their way across a scary bridge of belief. What do you say and do to keep them moving forward? It's a delicate process. You certainly don't shout at them or shove them. You don't want them to become distracted or suspicious. Instead you acknowledge their feelings. You provide freedom and guidance. And you send consistent and familiar signals to make everything appear unambiguous and safe.

Making us comfortable is about keeping our feeling minds fully engaged through rich associations—with stories, symbols, imagery and characters. Yet, at the same time, appeasing our skeptical thinking minds by making everything appear familiar and comforting, easy to interpret and accept.

Vikram Gandhi is an Indian-American filmmaker from New Jersey.

He was raised in a strict Hindu family, but felt no connection to his parent's Old World traditions.

Gandhi decided to make a documentary about the yoga industry in the United States.

He wanted to expose its "gurus."

The same types of spiritual phonies he encountered on a trip to India.

So he came up with an idea.

He would turn himself into a fake guru and create a *real* following of spiritual seekers.

Then, in a big cinematic reveal, he'd expose the whole thing as a ruse.

So, he grew a beard and flowing hair.

He adopted a high-pitched Indian accent.

He invented nonsensical, yet convincing symbols and rituals.

He even hired two female accomplices to pose as groupies and spread the word (one was a genuine yoga instructor).

Then he donned saffron robes and sandals, and headed west to Arizona.

He figured "people there would be open to the teachings of an Eastern guru."

And no one would recognize him.

Gandhi, as Kumaré, was a happy and positive guru.

He made deep eye contact and validated people's feelings with a gentle, childlike approach.

And it worked.

Because Gandhi understood that creating belief is about affect before effect.

It's about finding people who want to believe, and then making them feel comfortable.

Correct in their assumptions through the right signals and associations.

Like how marketers align their retail brands with our unconscious assumptions.

They know that we're very busy shoppers.

That we scan the shelves, searching for images and information which are congruent with our beliefs.

So they choose location, packaging and presentation to connect with our existing network of associations.

To gently pull us towards *our* values and desires.

So that we ultimately choose *their* products.

Just like Vikram Gandhi did with his audience.
And his brand called Kumaré.

Paint the Picture

People don't venture down an unfamiliar path, unless they can visualize *their desired destination*. I emphasize those words, because most people make erroneous assumptions about others—inferences that are colored by their own points of view.

For example, many are under the impression that selling people on the reasons why they should make a particular decision—like the importance of a healthy diet—will be effective in influencing a change in behavior. But research has repeatedly shown that rational arguments are not very effective, since people's behavior is overwhelmed by *their* reasons—their beliefs and desires.

There are others who believe that people's behavior can be motivated with negative narratives—smokers with tracheotomies, soda drinkers guzzling down globs of fat, etc. This misguided notion assumes that gaining understanding of an unwanted experience, albeit in an emotionally powerful way, is what creates belief and motivation. But no one desires what they *don't* want, including imagery and information about it. As Henny Youngman reportedly quipped,

"When I read about the evils of drinking, I gave up reading."

We hunger for direction and inspiration. We want what's important to us to get better—our bodies, work, home and relationships. We want to imagine ourselves transforming our lives, and the lives of others. We want to feel good about our evolving narratives. It's why we read books, scan the Internet, and flip through magazines. We're looking for the before and after stories. We want to feel the pull of possibility, of moving beyond our existing reality.

Konrad Adenauer observed, "We all live under the same sky, but we don't all have the same horizon." To discover someone else's motivation, and bring it to life in a provocative way, is surprisingly difficult. Yet despite the fact that it's widely misunderstood, the essence of influencing others is simple.

People are drawn across the bridge of belief by their anticipation of a better experience and a better life. Effective leaders ignite people's imaginations by painting vivid, compelling, and personally relevant pictures—ones that move them. As John Quincy Adams made clear, "If your actions inspire others to dream more, learn more, do more and become more, you are a leader."

Dreams, not Nightmares

In 1988, the citizens of Chile were faced with a simple choice.

"Yes" to extend the rule of their military dictator, General Augusto Pinochet.

"No" to oust him.

Pinochet agreed to the national vote under pressure from the international community.

But he was confident it would go his way.

The opposition had only 15 minutes each night for a month to make their case on state-run TV.

And Pinochet would use that same time to hammer home his fear-based propaganda.

The opposition's instinct was to speak truth to power.

To spotlight Pinochet's crimes against his people.

Fortunately, they changed their minds.

Instead of airing grim TV spots showing brutality and suffering, they opted for a fresh and positive appeal.

An uplifting vision of Chile's future.

"Chile, happiness is coming!" ignited their imaginations.

It aroused feelings of freedom and optimism. And it helped move Chileans to vote "No" and restore democracy.

Make it Ours

There's a well-known quote, or some variation of it, that is often attributed to Mahatma Gandhi, "There go my people. I must follow them, for I am their leader." Great leaders are viscerally aware that they are simply guides on *our* trips, and so they do everything possible to make our journeys feel special by strategically pushing decisions and actions in our direction.

Why do we like to shop, but hate to be sold? Because shopping is ours, selling is theirs. It's the same reason we prefer our digital playlists to broadcast radio, and why we love our social networks (we control what gets shared). Our favorite teachers and coaches use their expertise to engage and involve us by asking for *our* opinions, and involving us in projects that interest *us*. And so do the best marketers, innovators and salespeople.

Making it ours is not giving us control of the ship. Rather, it's connecting the voyage—especially the questions, highlights and successes—to our desires and choices. Great leaders of all stripes make it ours by making us feel that we are at the center of things.

The National Football League is a whopping $9.5
billion annual business.
Mainly by making us feel like part of a tribe.
Cheeseheads, 49ers Faithful, The Sea of Red.
But *Fantasy* Football takes it deeper.
It makes it ours.
And as a result, it has exploded to over 30 million
participants and into a $800 million industry.
It's such a simple idea.
Give individuals the ability to assemble and manage
their own virtual teams of real players.
Then use the players' actual NFL game numbers to
determine outcomes in the fantasy league.
Instead of screaming our dissent at inept coaches, we
get to show off our expertise.
Of course, gambling is a large part of its appeal.
Players are lured by the fantasy of winning cash.
But the *real* fantasy of Fantasy Football lies in
making it ours.
Our idea. Our decisions. Our team. Our brand.
And with that shift in control and ownership, the
NFL players' success becomes our success as well.

Make it Easy

In 2010, Google CEO Eric Schmidt made an astonishing statement, "Every two days now we create as much information as we did from the dawn of civilization up until 2003." We live in an age of distraction, of overwhelming amounts of conflicting information and competing priorities. And these complications can easily derail our progress on the bridge of belief.

Belief requires focus. It demands that we follow the lead of our feeling mind, of our intuition and assumptions. Distractions and difficulties turn on our *thinking* mind, which undermines belief by overriding our instincts.

When we investigate a product and find confusing information, we walk away. When we click on a link and discover even more steps to make our purchase, we reconsider. If we have an idea to help our organization and imagine stifling bureaucracy, we shelf it. Even something as seemingly irrelevant as a hard to read font can cause us to lose touch with our intuition.

Great leaders simplify the belief process by eliminating difficulties and competing options on our attention. They work really hard to make belief really easy.

As Easy as Apple

Apple recovered from near death in 1997.

It's now one of the most valuable companies on Earth.

Because Steve Jobs made it easy for everyone to believe.

By focusing their attention.

First, by drastically reducing the number of products.

He cut dozens of computer models to four.

Then by eliminating company projects.

He'd ask his people for the *ten* things they should be working on, then slash their shortlist to *three*.

He pressed to make every product intuitive.

So easy to use, there'd be no need for a manual.

The first iPod had no on or off switch.

The iPhone was a breakthrough in simplicity.

The marketing for the iPad proclaimed, "You already know how to use it."

Apple's leaders even obsess over packaging.

Designers spend months testing hundreds of prototypes.

And the results are always beautifully evocative of the experience.

Attractive to the eye and easy on the brain.

Apple believes in making everything easy.

And that unwavering belief fostered people's belief in Apple.

Get Us to Act

Let's assume that we desire what's on the other side of the bridge—the picture is compelling. And we feel comfortable and in control—drawn by our instincts. But we may still be unsure. Is the bridge really as stable and safe as we've been led to believe?

Taking a step forward on the bridge reinforces our feeling of knowing that it will support us. That step also triggers our story-creating mind to change the way we see ourselves. Once we do something, it becomes part of who we are, and we support that identity with future thoughts and behavior.

Sports coaches influence our beliefs by helping us tweak our mechanics and performance. Marketers influence our beliefs by getting us to try their new products. Fundraisers move us by getting us to participate in the "community." Our parents encourage us to get back up on our bikes.

Belief is a result of experience and repetition—both within and without—which makes our actions feel familiar and safe. Great leaders help create those experiences by deliberately influencing our behavior.

Do teachers' beliefs influence how students perform?
Studies have confirmed that obvious question.
When teachers were led to believe that their students
were intellectually gifted, the students' performance
improved.
Because the teachers' behavior towards them
changed.
So how do we get teachers to have the right beliefs,
which will then create the right behaviors?
That's what Bob Pianta, dean of the Curry School of
Education at UVa, wanted to find out.
So he took some teachers and assessed their beliefs.
He then gave one group a teaching course, with
information about appropriate beliefs and behavior.
A different group received intensive behavioral
training with personal coaches.
They were evaluated on recorded video, and helped
to practice new teaching routines.
Pianta then reassessed the beliefs of all of the
teachers.
And he found that beliefs shifted far more with
behavioral training.

Marshall McLuhan argued, it's "experience rather than understanding that influences our behavior." And Bob Pianta has shown that it's behavior, rather than understanding, that best influences our beliefs.

Make Progress Visible

Behavior is a powerful influence on our feelings. But its affect will be short-lived, unless it is reinforced by our perceptions and experiences. Unless progress is made visible. Progress is movement in the direction of our desires. It's a sense of accomplishment. A validating feeling that, given a plethora of competing options, our decisions and behaviors are the right ones for us to be making. Effective leaders send signals that make those feelings salient—interactions that are tied directly to our behaviors.

Marketers strategically reward our loyalty. Coaches and teachers highlight and celebrate our positive behaviors and accomplishments. Designers surprise us with unexpected beauty and utility. Salespeople and fundraisers reinforce our self-esteem.

Call it what you will—rewarding behavior, celebrating small wins, or simply giving someone an attaboy—the intent is the same. To continually remind us that we've chosen the best possible course. To reinforce our beliefs by illuminating the bridge directly in front of our eyes.

Positive Tickets

How do you get at-risk youth to believe in good behavior?
Ward Clapham was stirred by that question.
So he took a chance and defied conventional wisdom.
Clapham was hired to lead the Royal Canadian Mounted Police in Richmond, British Columbia.
The third largest force in the country, and with its share of community problems caused by unruly kids.
Clapham decided to change the paradigm of policing.
Instead of catching kids doing something wrong, his officers would shine a light on kids who were doing something right.
By issuing "positive tickets"—citations that rewarded kids' good behavior with local perks.
A meal at a restaurant or a ticket to a theme park.
During his tenure, Clapham's officers issued three times as many "positive tickets" as violations.
And youth-related incidents plummeted.

Because Ward Clapham had a vision of a caring community.

One that encouraged at-risk kids to stay on an admirable bridge of belief.

It's not enough to simply know that we're on the right path in life.

We must also feel and be affected by it.

Exude Passion

You've probably seen someone talking about something they know about. But have you ever seen someone *being* what they're talking about? There's a profound difference, one that creates a magnetic attraction. And that difference is passion—a rare combination of confidence and energy.

When we think about individuals who exude passion, we tend to envision intense, charismatic personalities like John F. Kennedy and Dr. Martin Luther King, Jr. But it's not an impressive title, physical dominance, or soaring rhetoric that creates belief. It's an inspiring vision and steadfast resolve.

Exuding passion is not about creating a carefully honed image. It's about making a statement about your values and convictions—the bigger cause that drives you. Competence, confidence, warmth, and enthusiasm, in both words and actions, are what move people today.

Yes, we experience passion in the consistent words and purpose-driven actions of our leaders. But it also manifests as an outpouring of innovative new products, bold and engaging communication, and, especially, in the deeply held beliefs and behaviors of others like us.

Whether it's launching a new product, making a presentation, crafting a press release, or asking for help, your best argument is always yourself—*your* exuberance, *your* vitality, *your* passion, your belief.

Passion is Infectious

Anjezë Gonxhe Bojaxhiu left her home at the age of 18 to pursue her bigger cause.

50 years later she was awarded the Nobel Peace Prize.

4'10" tall Mother Teresa was passion personified.

She had a steadfast belief in her work.

And the confidence to boldly express those feelings in her words and actions.

One time, she was on a flight to Mexico City.

When her lunch came, she asked how much it cost.

"Around a dollar," replied the puzzled flight attendant.

"If I give the meal back to you," asked Mother Teresa, "will you give me the money for the poor?"

The attendant checked and agreed to Mother's request.

Witnessing what had happened, the others near her gave up their meals in exchange for the money for Mother Teresa.

And that sentiment spread to every single person on the plane.

But that was not nearly enough for Mother Teresa.

As the plane was landing, and with everyone's meal money in hand, she asked for something else.

She wanted the forgone meals as well.

For the poor.

There's an old Hasidic saying, "The man who has confidence in himself gains the confidence of others."

That's true, but only if he's willing to express that confidence with boldness, with passion.

Control Their Impulses

The philosopher Alan Watts once remarked, "If you put your hand on the knee of a beautiful woman and leave it there, she'll cease to notice it. But if you gently pat her on the knee, she'll know you're still there. Because you come and you go. Now you see me, now you don't." Effective leaders know when to come and when to go; when to be heard and seen, and when to disappear and remain silent. They know how to control their mental impulses.

Impulses are the feeling mind trying to motivate some type of behavior, typically a rapid, unplanned action like jumping back when you think you've seen a snake. It's a great observer and pointer, but it's a horrible leader. It's easily distracted. It seeks instant gratification. It wants its fears overcome and desires met right away. And it has little concern for the consequences of its actions.

Great leaders know when to say "no" to their feeling minds and use their thinking mind—their brain's executive function—to manage impulses and make thoughtful decisions. They have a long-term view of their journeys, and so carefully consider the meaning behind each and every word, symbol and action.

Controlling impulses is more encompassing than face-to-face interactions, like putting away your phone when in the presence of others. Or knowing when to hold your tongue, soften your facial expression and listen with empathy. It involves all aspects of communication—verbal and nonverbal, direct and indirect—like knowing how quickly to answer an email, or whether, and when, to respond to the press.

Sales professionals know when to proffer information and when to hold back, when to follow up and when to lie low. Skilled marketers are attuned to the appropriate timing and frequency of communication and promotions. The very best designers know exactly what types of signals to send and when. And so do the best teachers, coaches and managers, who provide encouragement and critical feedback precisely when it's needed.

There's a fine art to balancing the need for feedback and results, and empowering others to focus and advance their own journeys. Great leaders skillfully walk that tightrope by strategically controlling their impulses.

Calm the Baton

Years ago, I had the pleasure of spending some time with the music director and conductor Ben Zander. Ben told me that orchestra musicians, like people in general, have a natural inclination to "spiral down." Over time, their vibrancy and energy tend to trail off.

The leader's job is to pull them back up.

To remind them of the rhythm of transformation.

I thought of that time while listening to an interview with the violin prodigy Joshua Bell.

In 2011, Bell was appointed Music Director and conductor of the Academy of St Martin in the Fields. Bell said that as a musician, he's worked with good and bad conductors.

And he affirmed Zander's sentiment that the good ones help unify the musicians and create excitement. The bad ones, he noted, "get in the way of the music."

The bad ones "give cues that are contrary to what's intuitive for the musician."

And every time the bad ones have a thought, "they stop the orchestra and say it."

Bell humbly acknowledged that he's still learning, especially when he "should not give a cue and just let the musicians play."

"When you're not showing every single thing that you have on your mind," he added, "then when you do show something, it makes so much more of an impact."

And as Bell, Zander, and all great leaders know, impact is the name of today's game.

Hide the How

Napoleon observed that "a leader is a dealer in hope." But he didn't make that glaring statement to his people. Great leaders influence stealthily and downplay their roles. They hide the how. They understand that belief is driven by our senses and by our feeling minds, and that we're moved by our imagined stories and experiences. And so they work hard to bring those mental images to life, to elevate our energy and instigate change by making experiences *feel* personal and transformative.

This is a difficult concept to get across with words. It's like trying to describe the intricate and lengthy illusion woven into the creation of an award-winning movie. It's impossible to do, and it misses the essential point of the experience—the emotional truth.

The fact is, we really don't want to *think* about what went into our favorite movies, just like we don't want to think about the reality behind most of our beliefs. Great leaders know this, and so they carefully orchestrate the drama to hide the how, to conceal the magic and inner workings of our journey.

I know that sashimi is cold, dead fish.

I know that my donation to the starving child in the advertisement probably isn't sent directly to that child.

And I know that the service representative on the phone isn't really thankful that I called.

I know that my government is holding back information about impending threats.

I know the economy is built on little more than belief.

I know that the guy who sold me my new car appeases me, so that he can sell me my next one.

I know that spraying on my designer fragrance doesn't make me irresistible.

And I know that those nutritional supplements I ingest may not be doing a darn bit of good.

I know that the company I just hired, the one behind the elegantly designed website, is probably just one guy in a home office.

I know that the Dalai Lama's shaved head and saffron robe have nothing to do with his compassionate heart.

And I know that a coyote can run twice as fast as a
roadrunner.

I know all of those things and more.

I just don't want to have them pointed out to me.

As the film director Errol Morris recently made clear,

"People despise reality, but love verisimilitude."

Summary of What They Do

W. Edwards Deming wrote, "If you can't describe what you are doing as a process, you don't know what you are doing." Effective leaders know precisely what they are doing. And the very first thing they do is choose a particular audience and develop a visceral understanding of their beliefs and, especially, their desires.

That may sound like common sense, but I can assure you that it's not. Skipping (or skimping on) that essential first step underlies the failure of most new products and businesses, as well as the struggles of a host of entrepreneurs, teams and organizations.

Once leaders empathize and understand us, they take us on an engaging mental journey. One that appeals to our beliefs and desires. And one with a carefully crafted and motivating picture of possibility and transformation. A journey designed to draw us in and move us forward by making us feel comfortable, invested and in complete control.

It's a skillful blend of passion, creativity, self-awareness and impulse control. As Lao-Tzu wrote in the "Tao Te Ching":

Learn from the people
Plan with the people
Begin with what they have
Build on what they know
Of the best leaders
When the task is accomplished
The people will remark
We have done it ourselves.

Part Three:
What You Can Do

Be More Conscious

Carl Jung noted, "Until you make the unconscious conscious, it will direct your life and you will call it fate." Now, you may *call* it fate, but it's not. Whether you're trying to influence others, or trying to influence your own life, the result of your choices—consciously made or habitual—is called destiny.

We have no control over fate. Fate chooses us, like our birthplace, our physical attributes or getting a flat tire on a rainy day. It determines our situation, who we "are" at that moment. But fate does not determine how we react, who we will "be." We do. We choose how we play the hand we're dealt, and those choices are what determine our destiny in life.

We can either allow ourselves to be pulled along through life by our instincts and habits, by our impulsive, feeling mind. Or we can slow down and be more conscious of our choices. To have any influence at all over our futures, or the futures of others, we must stop believing everything we think and question the validity of our lazy assumptions. We must break the happy trance of our present beliefs and create new thinking patterns.

The Real Definition of Insanity

During a recent conversation, my daughter crowned an argument by reciting a popular saying.
"The definition of insanity is doing the same thing over and over and expecting different results."
Clever kid.
"Perhaps," I replied.
"But isn't it also insane to do the same thing over and over and expect the *same* results?"
She was dumbfounded.
I was being quite sincere.
What happens to experts and most other comfortable people?
We end up making the conscious *unconscious*.
Our beliefs become fossilized and seduce us to continue "our ways."
Our existing knowledge and situation dulls our senses to the reality of the changing world.
Our minds become protected by layers of fat we call experience.
And we rationalize our habits for dealing with the world—doing the same things over and over—with our comfort and brilliant achievements.

This self-reinforcing delusion is the real definition of insanity.

We're insane to think we can save or consume our way to peace and happiness.

We're insane to believe we can control people or work them to the brink of meltdown with no blowback.

We're insane to imagine that we can ravage the Earth to our hearts' content.

We're insane to focus on the urgent at the expense of the important.

And we're insane to use the same thinking and methods and expect wildly different results.

Have you been doing pretty much the same things over and over?

Does it feel compulsive and unsatisfying?

Then stop.

Get out of your office.

Leave your store.

Step away from the factory.

Turn off your computer.

Heaven forbid, power off your cell phone.

And open your child-like eyes to the reality of the world.

Watch and really wonder.

Question and fully explore.

Your mind will come alive and it will melt the self-imposed fat of prejudice and routine.

Your unconscious will become conscious.

And you will become sane again.

Ignore It

If you have an idea, any idea, and you Google it, you will inevitably find it. I found that more than 11,000 new business books are published each year, and most sell fewer than a thousand copies. This instant access to information about everyone and everything is having a deadly effect on our confidence. It's shutting down the childlike optimism required to pursue a new belief. The data is clear, so why take the risk?

But the real risk isn't found in the data. It's the risk of not fully living during our one trip around the track. It's the risk of regret. So ignore it. The great sociologist Emile Durkheim wrote, "A mind that questions everything, unless strong enough to bear the weight of its ignorance, risks questioning itself and being engulfed in doubt."

No one can predict the future. Hindsight is required to tell us what works and what doesn't. And while we're waiting for the conditions to be just right, the beauty and excitement of life is flying right on by. So ignore all of that doubt-inducing information and be driven by curiosity and passion. Have the wisdom and courage to follow your heart.

Here's the truth.

You are not your history.

And, if you're working on something, someone else on the planet is working on something very similar.

I distinctly remember an interview with the writer Vince Gilligan.

Gilligan is the creative mind behind "Malcolm in the Middle," the "X-Files," and the hit movie "Hancock."

Here's what he said about his acclaimed television series "Breaking Bad."

The idea sprung into his head fully-formed, "somewhat in an instant."

He was amazed that he even pitched the idea and that it's on the air, since "on paper it should not work."

He's glad he didn't know about the existence of the TV series "Weeds" (a similar idea).

Had he known about "Weeds," he "would have never gone forward and pitched 'Breaking Bad.'"

So forget who you were.

Forget what you've done.

And forget what others are doing (don't Google it!).

Simply ask, What am I passionate about?

Now go do that.

And bingo!

That's who you are.

Flip Your Lid

For most of us, seeing is believing. We are moved by our perceptions, by our immediate concerns and desires, and not by our hopes and dreams of a better future. It's the default mode of our mental operating system (perception-cognition-belief-decision). We allow our present "reality" to inform our instinctive, self-concerned mind, which then drives our feelings, thoughts, beliefs and decisions.

Today, more than ever before, we're hooked on the visible—short-term stimulation that's injected directly into our brains. If you want to change your life, you must reverse the order of that default-setting. Instead of being driven by your senses, be driven by a belief—in something bigger and better. Or, as Stephen Covey advised, "Begin with the end in mind."

Make the decision first and allow that choice to direct your thoughts, and inform your instincts, your feelings and perceptions (decision-belief-cognition-perception). When you do, others will not be able to highjack your mind and move you along a bridge of unfavorable consequences.

Believing is Seeing

Do you know that it's impossible to hit a major
league fastball?

Let's do the math.

It takes 250 milliseconds for the muscles, bones and
tendons of an elite athlete to take a full swing.

The visual reaction time——the time is takes to see
the ball and mentally respond to it——is 200
milliseconds.

Now, add those two times together.

The sum is the time it takes for a batter to see
(perception), feel, think (cognition) and swing
(decision and action).

A full 450 milliseconds.

But here's the problem.

A fastball travels from the pitcher's hand to the
catcher's mitt in just *400* milliseconds.

50 milliseconds quicker than the batter's perception-
cognition-action biology.

So how do they do it?

They flip common sense.

They reverse the order of their evolutionary
programming.

Instead of allowing perception—their present reality
—to drive their actions, they begin with belief.
They're not driven by their senses.
Instead, they're driven by a *sense* of purpose.
A philosophy and guiding approach (belief).
Then they turn on their *thinking* minds and master
the details of that approach (cognition).
They study and practice until it shifts their
perception.
Until it creates new muscle memory and becomes
second nature.
And finally—and only then—they allow their
instincts and senses to advise them.
To filter information and inform their framework
(perception).
They don't have to think about every decision,
because their beliefs have trained their perception.
It *is* impossible to hit a major league fastball (try it).
Yet those driven by their beliefs are busy warming
up for another day on their field of dreams.
Because they've flipped their lids.
They've reversed their default mental programming.
They've discovered that breakthrough achievement
is about belief, then perception.
Conviction, then action.

Magic, then logic.
Heart, then head.
They know that seeing isn't believing.
Believing is seeing.

Behave to Believe

When I was a boy, my father told me that I could do anything in life, so long as I put my mind to it. I now know that his guidance wasn't literally true (I still can't dunk a basketball). But I have discovered the hidden wisdom in his words. Since I grew up believing that I could do just about anything, I ended up trying a lot of things. And those simple acts of doing had a profound effect on my subsequent beliefs and decisions.

Pascal argued that by acting *as if* one believed, one would end up believing. Two centuries later, William James declared, "If you want a quality, act *as if* you already had it." In other words, don't try to *think* your way to a change, to positive mental states like happiness or confidence. Act *as if*, by changing your behavior, and your actions will convince your mind.

I once heard a seminar leader exclaim, "*You* control your attitude!" What she meant was, "Control your thoughts, people." But, as we've discovered, that's much easier said than done. Instead, *influence* your attitude by controlling your actions. Change your behavior and your behavior will change your mind.

Snap Out of It!

A while back, following a keynote speech and during Q&A, someone in the audience asked a heartfelt, yet somewhat rhetorical question.

"So, how do I communicate to people that our approach, our culture, needs to change?"

My immediate impulse was to hit her with a stick.

Like Zen masters reportedly would do to knock someone out of her attachment to conventional reasoning.

But I was on a stage and far from her.

And anyway, I didn't have a stick.

So, I gave her a koan-like question to ask "those people."

A seemingly self-evident one designed to snap them out of it, to open their minds.

"Ask them if your organization, your culture, is producing the results it is designed to produce?"

As I glanced around the auditorium for a reaction, all I could sense was collective confusion.

And their visceral desire to shout out the, apparently, obvious response.

"Of course it's not, idiot.

Otherwise, she wouldn't have asked you that question."

But no one dared blurt that out.

Instead, they just sat there, perplexed.

Why? Because they were deluded.

They believed that their organization was NOT producing the results it was designed to produce.

And they assumed that the reason had something to do with their people, with them.

In fact, their organization is producing precisely the results it is designed to produce.

So is yours.

So is your community, your family, your government, your country.

So is your life.

Because . . . the design determines the results.

So snap out of it!

Stop fighting the existing reality.

Stop trying to change the people.

Stop trying to change your mind.

If you don't like the results, change the design.

The great systems theorist and designer Buckminster Fuller put it this way.

"You never change things by fighting the existing reality.
To change something, build a new model that makes the existing model obsolete."
To change your beliefs, change your behavior.

Stay Passionate!

I'll never forget an enlightening conversation with college friends back in the economic heydays of the 90s. It has stuck with me for all these years and often helps inform my decision-making, especially during uncertain times like these.

As we relaxed and enjoyed a Labor Day cookout, and our good health and fortune, I spurted out that I was, once again, venturing into the great marketplace unknown. At the time we were all disengaged yet seemingly secure in executive positions with established organizations, unquestioningly embracing the status quo.

Upon hearing my news, one bewildered friend glanced at me, shook his head from side to side, and professed, "I could never do what you do."
"What's that?" I asked.
"You know," he answered, pausing to sip his imported beer. "Risking it all."
"Risking it all?" I replied. "It's *you* who are 'risking it all.' And for what it's worth," I continued. "I could never do what you guys are doing."

What they were doing, what many are still doing, was playing it safe instead of playing it with passion. And by "playing it with passion," I don't mean "following" ones passion. I've never "followed my passion," because, frankly, I have no idea what my singular passion is.

Perhaps it's why I'm so amused by comedian Mitch Hedberg's absurd declaration: "I'm sick of following my dreams, man. I'm just going to ask where they're going and hook up with 'em later." But why follow them? Why hook up with them? Why not be the leader of your life and let your dreams hook up with you?

Don't be confused. It's really simple: Your life's purpose is the quality of your life's experiences. Living life with passion *is* following your passion. Unfortunately, most people believe that passion will mysteriously appear, or that the purpose of life is the pursuit of comfort. They view life as a waiting game with a series of problems to avoid, rather than an exciting game with the clock ticking and opportunities to pursue.

Comfort is an illusion; a fantasy that imagines freedom from pain and suffering if only we stay still and avoid change. What most fail to realize, typically until it's very late in the game, is that change happens to us whether we like it or not.

G. K. Chesterton wrote, "If you leave a thing alone you leave it to a torrent of change. If you leave a white post alone it will soon be a black post. If you particularly want it to be white you must be always painting it again; that is, you must be always having a revolution."

Without intervention, without progressive change, without revolution, everything in our work and our lives gets worse. Our bodies degrade, our relationships fizzle, our jobs disappear, and our ideas become obsolete (it has happened to countless organizations and to most of my friends).

Face it: We are either breaking out of our spirit-sucking routines and breaking through to new insights and experiences, or we are breaking down. So when the opportunity to step out of your comfort zone arrives, and it will definitely come, take it. Say no to the sure thing and say yes to a creative challenge. Say no to short-term, comfort producing activities, and say yes to fear, passion and leader-ship.

What Ever Happened to Dreams?

Jake was a typical teenager.

Overweight.

Insecure.

A bit soft and naive.

Then one day, he had a dream.

One in which he felt energetic, powerful, self-assured.

That dream stirred Jake.

It created a hunger that demanded to be fed.

So he started going to the gym.

He ran on the treadmill.

He lifted weights.

His mind was on fire with visions of change, of success.

He read everything he could get his hands on, sought out role models, and asked for help.

He worked hard, really really hard.

He tried new exercises.

He modified his routines and his diet.

And slowly, but surely, it worked.

Jake's desire and discipline transformed him.

His dream became his reality.

Then one day, Jake forgot how to dream.
When he looked at the weights he saw the reality of pain, not the instruments of possibility.
He became bored and comfortable.
He wanted to relax, to cruise for a while.
So he searched out information and voices that validated his new desire.
And he found them.
Jake breathes easier now.
He's created an environment and routine that make him feel good.
And so, he's done growing.
Jake reminds me of so many people and organizations.
Jake was moved by a dream, by a burning desire to create a new future.
And so he grew.
But then he became contented.
Tired of the hard work and tedium of the fundamentals.
So now he dabbles with new fangled approaches.
He rationalizes his feel good routines.
He talks dispassionately, like an accountant.
Jake has matured.
He's smart.

He's a realist.

And his impassioned dream is nothing but a fond and distant memory.

J.R.R. Tolkien wrote, "A single dream is more powerful than a thousand realities."

Reality is for wimps.

About the Author

Tom Asacker writes and teaches about radically new practices and ideas for marketplace success in times of uncertainty and change. He is the author of six groundbreaking books that redefine business for the new millennium.

A popular speaker, Tom has lectured on marketing, innovation, and marketplace trends to corporate, association, and university audiences around the world. As an independent business consultant, he's advised start-up ventures, NPOs, and Fortune 500 companies on innovation, emerging trends, and strategic communication and brand development.

Prior to his role as a writer, professional speaker and corporate catalyst, Tom was an agitator in management posts at GE and throughout his entrepreneurial endeavors as founder of a strategic brand consultancy, owner of an electronics manufacturing firm, and co-founder and CEO of a medical device company.

Visit www.tomasacker.com for more information, and for interviews or booking information.

Made in the USA
Charleston, SC
20 January 2014